THE ENVIRONMENT CHALLENGE

SUSTAINING OUR NATURAL RESOURCES

Jen Green

Chicago, Illinois

© 2011 Raintree
an imprint of Capstone Global Library, LLC
Chicago, Illinois

Visit our website at www.heinemannraintree.com

Edited by Andrew Farrow and Adam Miller
Designed by Victoria Allen
Original illustrations © Capstone Global Library Ltd.
Illustrated by Tower Designs UK Limited
Picture research by Mica Brancic
Production by Camilla Crask
Originated by Capstone Global Library Ltd.
Printed and bound in China by South China Printing Company.

15 14 13 12 11
10 9 8 7 6 5 4 3 2 1

Library of Congress Cataloging-in-Publication Data
Green, Jen.
  Sustaining our natural resources / Jen Green.
    p. cm.—(The environment challenge)
  Includes bibliographical references and index.
  ISBN 978-1-4109-4300-2 (hb freestyle)—ISBN 978-1-4109-4307-1 (pb freestyle) 1. Conservation of natural resources—Juvenile literature. 2. Renewable energy resources—Juvenile literature. 3. Sustainable development—Juvenile literature. I. Title.
  S940.G74 2012
  333.95'16—dc22   2010052725

ISBNs:
978-1-4109-4300-2 (HC)
978-1-4109-4307-1 (PB)

Acknowledgments
The author and publishers are grateful to the following for permission to reproduce copyright material: Alamy p. 37 © Inga Spence, p. 38 © Jim West, p. 39 © AGStockUSA; Corbis p. 4 © Greg Smith, p. 7 © Frédéric Soltan, p. 8 © Gerhard Egger, p. 11 © Gerald French, p. 15 © Paul Souders, p. 21 © Tom Bean, p. 22 © Gerd Ludwig, p. 24 Science Faction/© Karen Kasmauski, p. 26 Reuters/© Tomas Bravo, p. 27 © Andrew Holbrooke, p. 28 Rubberball/© Mike Kemp, p. 30 JAI/© Nigel Pavitt, p. 31 © Karen Kasmauski, p. 35 Reuters/© Nicky Loh, p. 41 © Juice Images; Getty Images p. 12 Iconica/ Frans Lemmens, p. 14 National Geographic/Michael Nichols; p. 17 Robert Nickelsberg, p. 18 AFP Photo/Khaled Desouki, p. 19 Mike Goldwater, p. 23 National Geographic/Tim Laman, p. 25 Stockbyte, p. 29 Bloomberg/Adeel Halim, p. 32 AFP Photo/Elmer Martinez, p. 33 Bloomberg/Mike Mergen, p. 40 AFP Photo/Boris Horvat; Photolibrary p. 36 Animals Animals/Glenn Vanstrum; Reuters p. 34 Shannon Stapleton; Shutterstock p. 5 © Eugene Suslo, p. 10 © Gary Whitton, p. 13 © Jim Parkin.

Cover photograph of woman's hands planting a seedling in Hebei, China, is reproduced with the permission of Corbis/© Yi Lu.

We would like to thank Michael D. Mastrandrea, Ph.D. for his invaluable help in the preparation of this book.

Every effort has been made to contact copyright holders of any material reproduced in this book. Any omissions will be rectified in subsequent printings if notice is given to the publisher.

Disclaimer
All the Internet addresses (URLs) given in this book were valid at the time of going to press. However, due to the dynamic nature of the Internet, some addresses may have changed, or sites may have changed or ceased to exist since publication. While the author and publisher regret any inconvenience this may cause readers, no responsibility for any such changes can be accepted by either the author or the publisher.

Contents

Words appearing in the text in bold, **like this**, are explained in the glossary.

Natural Resources and Sustainability

Researching information

Throughout this book, you will find ideas for further research. You could use a number of different sources. Libraries have books, records, and access to the Internet. Newspapers and television reports often present the facts clearly, but they may oversimplify things to make good headlines. The Internet is a valuable source of up-to-date information, but not all websites are reliable. So, try to find two independent sources. If they say different things, try to find a third!

Did you know that there were once over 20 million square kilometers (8 million square miles) of tropical rain forest worldwide? But, because humans have cleared these forests over time, less than half that area of tropical rain forest now remains.

All living things, including people, need natural **resources** like these rain forests for survival. Thanks to these natural resources, Earth has sustained life for over 3.5 billion years. But people are now using up many important resources faster than they can be replaced.

Using up nonrenewable resources

Many of the natural resources people most depend on are **nonrenewable**, meaning they will eventually get used up. This is especially true of **fossil fuels** like coal, oil, and natural gas. These important energy sources power everything, from our cars to the heat in our homes. But they take millions of years to form, so once they are gone, we cannot replace them. The burning of fossil fuels also causes **pollution** (harmful waste) and damages the environment.

Like all fossil fuels, coal took millions of years to form.

Cutting down forests

Timber from forests, another important natural resource, is used as a fuel and as a building material. Sometimes forests are also cleared for farming or to raise cattle. These forests are **renewable**, meaning they can be naturally replaced—new trees can be planted. However, once forests are cut down, it takes hundreds of years for new trees to grow into mature forests. Cutting down forests also damages the environment.

Damaging environment resources

Air, water, and soil support living things. They are seemingly limitless natural resources. Similarly, plants, animals, and other living things are nature's food sources. They replace themselves through reproduction, so they are also renewable.

However, many of these environmental resources are in danger because of human activities. Pollution is making the air, water, and soil unsafe, and it is killing off many kinds of living things. As humans build and expand into new areas, the plants and animals that once lived there are also harmed and sometimes killed off forever.

Clearly, our overuse of natural resources is placing great strain on the environment. So, how can we find a path forward that does not use up all of Earth's natural resources?

Wind turbines like these use a limitless, renewable source of energy: the wind. This sort of technology could help solve our reliance on nonrenewables (see pages 12 and 13).

(see pages 12 and 13).

WORD BANK

fossil fuel	fuel such as coal, oil and natural gas that is made of fossilized plants or animals
nonrenewable	describes resources, such coal and oil, that will get used up
pollution	when the natural world is harmed by waste or any substance that does not belong there

What is sustainability?

"Sustainability" means using Earth's resources in a planned and careful way. This approach will meet our present needs, while preserving resources for the future. The basic idea is simple. If we use resources faster than they can be replaced, they will get completely used up.

Sustainable development

Sustainability is a fairly new idea, dating back to the 1980s. Before that, few people thought about the need to preserve Earth's resources, because they seemed limitless. Then, **environmentalists** (people who work to help the environment) realized that resources such as oil, coal, and forests were limited and would one day run out.

So, scientists came up with the idea of **sustainable development**. This means managing economic growth and the way we live, without destroying resources that will be needed for the future.

Rising population

In the last 150 years, the human **population** (number of people) has grown rapidly. In 1900 there were 1.6 billion people on Earth. By 1999 there were 6 billion, and 7 billion people are expected by 2011. Every year there are more mouths to feed, and more fossil fuels, timber, and other resources are used to make all the things we want or need.

World population growth

Year	Population
1750	700,000,000
1804	1,000,000,000
1850	1,200,000,000
1900	1,600,000,000
1927	2,000,000,000
1950	2,550,000,000
1955	2,800,000,000
1960	3,000,000,000
1965	3,300,000,000
1970	3,700,000,000
1975	4,000,000,000
1980	4,500,000,000
1985	4,850,000,000
1990	5,300,000,000
1995	5,700,000,000
1999	6,000,000,000
2006	6,500,000,000
2009	6,800,000,000
2011	7,000,000,000
2025	8,000,000,000
2050	9,200,000,000

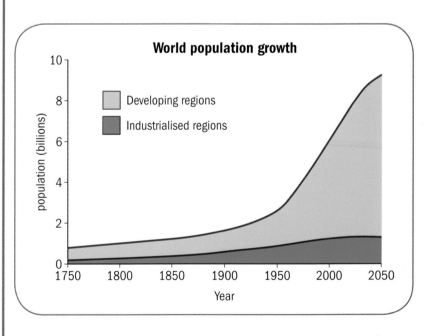

The chart (left) and graph (above) show the estimated rise in human population from 1750 to now, and how much it is expected to increase by 2050.

"Our American way of life—300+ million people enjoying historically unprecedented living standards—is NOT **sustainable** because the ecological resources and economic resources upon which it depends will not be available going forward."

Chris Clugston, Post Carbon Institute

This family is sorting through waste in a slum in Mumbai, India. According to the aid organization UNICEF, 24,000 children under five years old die each day due to poverty.

The five Ws

Over the course of your research, you will come across many different sources. Five simple questions will help you to judge the usefulness of each source: Who, What, When, Where, and Why? (These are sometimes called the "five Ws.") For example, ask: Who is the author? Is he or she an expert? What was the author's purpose in writing? Does he or she work for an organization that might want to put over a particular viewpoint? When and where was the text written? Is it up-to-date? Is the author giving hard facts or an opinion? Why is the text useful?

Ecological footprint

Environmentalists use the term "**ecological footprint**" to measure the impact our use of natural resources is having on the planet. The footprint compares individual countries' use of resources with the area needed to provide those resources. It is also used to measure total world use of resources.

In 2008 experts said the global ecological footprint was 1.4 Earths. That means that across the world, we were using Earth's resources 1.4 times faster than they could be replaced.

Sharing Earth's resources

But all countries are not using Earth's resources equally. People in wealthy countries like the United States and the United Kingdom, known as **developed countries**, consume vast amounts of resources such as food and fossil fuels.

At the same time, people in countries in poorer places like Africa and South America, known as **developing countries**, use 30 to 40 times fewer resources. In 2006 experts calculated that 1.8 hectares (4.6 acres) of land was needed to sustain every person in China, while every person in the United States needed 9.0 hectares (22.3 acres).

In developed countries, we all need to live less wastefully, so that we use fewer resources. People in developing countries need to get a fairer share of Earth's resources. This book will explore ways to achieve these goals.

This book will also explore humans' use and abuse of the planet's resources. As you read, take the environment challenge. Think closely about all sides of the issues and decide on the best way forward. How can we learn to not use up all of Earth's valuable resources?

In developed countries, we consume more than our fair share of Earth's resources. We also generate huge amounts of waste.

Ecological Debt Day

Ecological Debt Day is another way of looking at how quickly the planet's resources are being used up. The debt day is calculated to be the date on which we effectively use up all the resources that were available for that year. Once we hit this point, we start using up Earth's stock of resources.

Experts believe that before 1986, our total use of the planet's resources was outweighed by Earth's ability to generate new resources. A balance was maintained every year. But in 1987 we used up our supply of resources by December 19. In 2000 the date was November 1. Every year, the date moves a little closer to the start of the year. Find out more at the Global Footprint Network, at www.footprintnetwork.org/en/index.php/GFN/page/earth_overshoot_day/.

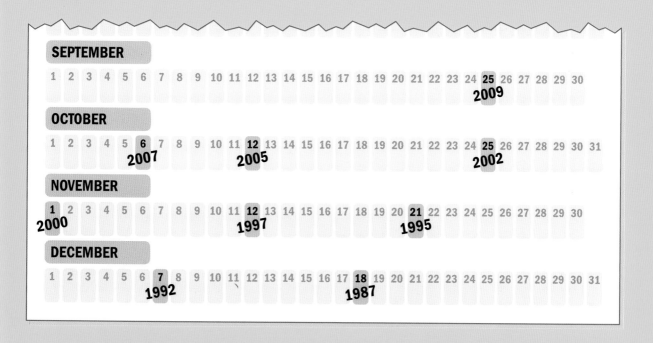

SEPTEMBER

1 2 3 4 5 6 7 8 9 10 11 12 13 14 15 16 17 18 19 20 21 22 23 24 **25** 26 27 28 29 30
2009

OCTOBER

1 2 3 4 5 **6** 7 8 9 10 11 **12** 13 14 15 16 17 18 19 20 21 22 23 24 **25** 26 27 28 29 30 31
2007　　　**2005**　　　　　　　　　　　　　　**2002**

NOVEMBER

1 2 3 4 5 6 7 8 9 10 11 **12** 13 14 15 16 17 18 19 20 **21** 22 23 24 25 26 27 28 29 30
2000　　　　　**1997**　　　　　　　**1995**

DECEMBER

1 2 3 4 5 6 **7** 8 9 10 11 12 13 14 15 16 17 **18** 19 20 21 22 23 24 25 26 27 28 29 30 31
1992　　　　　　　**1987**

Nonliving Resources

Nonliving **resources** include rocks, **minerals**, and **fossil fuels** such as coal. Most, but not all, of these resources are **nonrenewable**. Extracting, transporting, and consuming these resources can cause a lot of **pollution**.

Mining

Mining involves extracting (removing) valuable materials from ground level or deep below the surface. This process helps people find a variety of useful materials, including:

- fossil fuels such as coal, oil, and natural gas (see pages 12 and 13)
- minerals such as gypsum (used to make plaster and cement)
- ores, which are minerals that contain useful metals such as copper, iron, and bauxite
- gemstones
- rock used in construction.

These substances generally form very slowly, and so they are nonrenewable.

Impact of mining

Mining often has a lasting impact on the environment. Surface mining involves stripping away the covering plant life, soil, and rock. Deep-level mining involves building shafts and tunnels underground.

Mining generates huge amounts of waste rock. Copper mining produces 99 tonnes (109 tons) of waste rock for every tonne (1.1 ton) of copper.

The Bingham Canyon Mine in Utah is the world's deepest open-pit mine. Strip mining like this leaves a lasting scar on the landscape.

Waste rock, known as **tailings**, may be heaped at the surface of the work site. Sometimes tailings are dumped into old work sites that have become empty pits. These pits often fill with water, forming lakes.

Minerals such as copper and uranium produce highly **toxic** (poisonous) waste, which can leak into the soil. These poisons can also end up in lakes filled with liquid tailings. Most countries have regulations to minimize how much mining can harm the environment, but the rules are not always enforced.

CASE STUDY

Mining disaster in the Philippines

In 1996 an accident at a copper mine in the Philippines, in Southeast Asia, caused an environmental disaster. The Marcopper Mining Corporation had dumped tailings in a lake formed from an abandoned pit. However, the lake's drainage system failed, causing 1.6 cubic meters (56.5 cubic feet) of tailings to spill into local rivers, killing all wildlife. A flood of toxic waste spread to nearby farmland, making crops unsafe to eat.

What would YOU do ?

Imagine you are the head of a mining company that has discovered a new supply of minerals in a remote region. The owners of your company need you to make a profit. How much time and money would you spend protecting the environment? Use books or the Internet to research ways to minimize harm to the environment.

The colored pools of water in this photo contain copper tailings.

WORD BANK
extract   remove from the earth
mineral   hard, naturally occurring substance. Minerals help to provide everything from cement to gold.

Fuels

Fuels provide energy for homes, **industry** (factories and power plants), and transportation. Fuels include solids such as wood and coal, liquids such as oil, gases such as methane, and "**flow resources**" such as winds and tides, which use natural movements to create energy.

Fossil fuels—including coal, oil, and natural gas—are the world's most important fuels, currently supplying about three-quarters of all our energy needs. However, fossil fuels are nonrenewable, and supplies of fossil fuels are already running low. Scientists believe there is enough coal to last another 200 years, but oil and gas reserves may run out in 50 to 70 years.

Oil companies are finding they must drill in increasingly remote locations, such as Alaska and on the seabed, to find oil. In 2010 deep-level drilling in the Gulf of Mexico caused a catastrophic oil spill that will harm the local environment for many years to come. Burning fossil fuels also releases very harmful air pollution, which is altering Earth's weather patterns (see pages 14 and 15). So, what are the alternatives?

The nuclear option

Nuclear energy involves processing a rare metal, uranium, in a site called a reactor. This process does not release the same harmful air pollution as burning fossil fuels. However, after it is used, uranium is radioactive, meaning it gives off harmful rays of energy. This uranium is highly dangerous, and it cannot be disposed of safely. There is also the risk of accidents.

Government scientists are investigating a process called nuclear fusion, which could provide cheap, clean energy in the future. But the research is very, very expensive.

Wood is one of the main sources of energy in **developing countries** such as Kenya.

This power plant in South Dakota produces a "biofuel" called ethanol. Biofuels are produced from plant material, so can be considered renewable because new crops can be grown.

Geothermal power in Iceland

Geothermal plants use the energy of hot rocks underground for heating and electricity. This renewable technology can be used in areas with volcanic activity such as Iceland, Japan, and New Zealand. In Iceland, five large geothermal plants heat 89 percent of homes and provide a quarter of the country's electricity.

Environmental Resources

Earth's air, water, and soil are essential for living things. However **industry**, farming, and other human activities are polluting these crucial **resources**, threatening lasting harm to the planet.

Earth's atmosphere

The **atmosphere** is an envelope of gases surrounding Earth. It protects us from harmful rays from the Sun and debris (broken bits) from space. The atmosphere mainly consists of the gases nitrogen (78 percent) and oxygen (21 percent). The remaining one percent is mostly the gas argon, with traces of hydrogen, carbon dioxide, methane, and other gases.

Small amounts of carbon dioxide and methane trap some of the Sun's heat in the atmosphere. This causes temperatures on Earth to rise and creates conditions suitable for life. This is called the **greenhouse effect**.

Changing climate

For thousands of years, the makeup of the atmosphere has remained fairly stable. However, in the last 200 years, we have added more carbon dioxide to the atmosphere. This is because carbon dioxide is released when **fossil fuels** like coal, oil, and natural gas are burned. Carbon dioxide is also released when forests are burned to clear land for farming. This release of gases is increasing the natural greenhouse effect, causing a rise in temperatures known as **global warming**.

People burn rain forests to clear land for raising cattle. This adds to the carbon dioxide in the atmosphere.

Effects of global warming and climate change

Due to global warming, the last 30 years have had some of the warmest temperatures on record. Polar ice has started to melt, with the melted water going into oceans. This is contributing to the rise in sea levels. These changes caused by global warming are called **climate change**.

In this century, scientists predict global warming will make weather patterns more variable, increasing the likelihood of natural disasters such as **droughts** (long periods without rain), floods, and hurricanes. Many governments are now working together to try to slow down climate change.

To do our part individually, we need to reduce our dependence on fossil fuels and turn to non-polluting **renewable** energy sources instead. In **developed countries**, we also need to use less energy (see pages 40 and 41).

Investigate the greenhouse effect

Investigate the greenhouse effect by placing a thermometer outdoors in the Sun for 10 minutes. Record the temperature, then move the thermometer into a greenhouse, or put it into a glass jar in the sunlight. Take another reading after 10 minutes and compare the two readings. The effects you observe caused by the greenhouse or glass are similar to the effects caused by carbon dioxide and methane in the atmosphere.

The world's glaciers are melting. The melted water adds to the volume of ocean water.

Earth's freshwater

Did you know that around 97 percent of all the water on Earth is salty? Of the remaining 3 percent that is freshwater, over two-thirds is locked up as ice. Nearly one-third is located in underground layers of rock called **aquifers**. This leaves just 0.5 percent in freshwater sources such as rivers, lakes, and swamps.

"Fresh water can no longer be considered a limitless resource."
World Wide Fund for Nature (WWF)

Freshwater is essential for wildlife and also for farming, industry, and cities. But 70 percent of all the water we use goes to farming. Because too much water is being **extracted**, rivers, lakes, and aquifers are running dry.

Wasting water

In developed countries, we also waste a lot of water. Scientists say everyone needs about 50 liters (13 gallons) of water a day for drinking, washing, and preparing food. In the United States, people use around 500 liters (132 gallons) a day. In very dry regions such as Africa, many people manage on 10 liters (2.6 gallons) a day.

How is so much water being wasted? A lot of water gets wasted through leaking pipes, dripping faucets, and taking long showers. At this rate, we are using water faster than rainfall and aquifers can produce it, while aquifers and rivers are drying up.

Huge amounts of water are needed to grow crops and raise livestock—about 1,550 liters (410 gallons) to grow 1 kilogram (2.2 pounds) of rice, and up to 100,000 liters (26,400 gallons) to produce 1 kilogram (2.2 pounds) of beef.

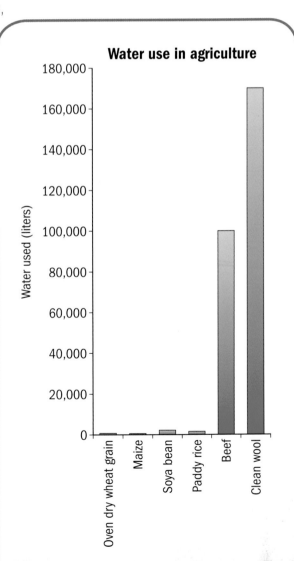

Pollution and growing pressure

Pollution from sewage (wastewater), farming, and industry dirties many freshwater sources. In 2009 the United Nations reported that 2.6 billion people worldwide lack adequate sanitation (wastewater removal), and nearly one billion are without clean water. Millions die from diseases such as dysentery, which is caused by drinking dirty water.

Across the world, we are overstraining water sources, and the pressure will grow as the **population** rises. Part of the answer is to improve water sources in places such as Africa. In developed countries, we need to waste less water.

People can get sick from drinking water that is also used for bathing or washing.

CASE STUDY

Shrinking Aral Sea

The Aral Sea in western Asia was once the world's fourth-largest lake. But starting in the 1960s, large-scale **irrigation** projects drew off huge amounts of water from the rivers flowing into the lake. Irrigation projects control the flow of water through channels and other devices. As a result of these projects, the lake has lost about 90 percent of its water, and local fisheries have collapsed.

WORD BANK
aquifer   layer of rock or earth underground that holds water
irrigation   method of controlling the flow of water through channels and other devices

Soil

Soil is a precious resource. It supports the plants that provide food for wildlife and humans. Soil takes many years to form, but it can easily be polluted by chemicals from factories or industry. Pollution lingers in the soil and is very difficult to remove.

Only about one-quarter of the world's land area is suitable for farming. The rest is too steep, stony, or dry. In dry parts of Africa, farmers often graze livestock on land bordering deserts where there is little rainfall. The animals can quickly strip existing plant life there faster than it can be replaced, making the land **barren** (producing no life). This can lead to **desertification**.

Chemicals from farming

Modern farming practices can harm the soil and the wider environment. In developed countries, most farmers use chemicals called **fertilizers** to improve harvests. When the chemicals drain into local streams and rivers, they cause tiny living things called algae and bacteria to multiply. This reduces oxygen levels in the water, killing wildlife such as fish.

Many farmers also use chemicals called pesticides to control weeds and insects. When these poisons wash into the ground, they can kill worms and other tiny living things that help keep the soil healthy.

Soil erosion

As the world population grows, the need for food increases. In response, farmers cut down forests and plow up grasslands to create more fields and pastureland. As they do so, they cut down trees and deep-rooted native plants that help to anchor the soil. When the ground is stripped bare in this way, it can quickly lead to **erosion**, meaning the soil is worn away.

In places such as Egypt, too much irrigation draws natural salts to the surface. The land can become too salty for farming.

Make a KWL chart

Using books or the Internet, find out more about the impact of farming on the soil. A KWL chart can help you organize your research. "K" stands for "What I **k**now"; "W" stands for "What I **w**ant to know"; and "L" stands for "What I **l**earned." Your main question goes in column 2. Fill in column 1 using the facts given here. New facts from your research go in column 3.

What I know	What I want to know	What I learned
Modern farming can damage the soil.	How does pollution affect living things in the soil?	

CASE STUDY

Expanding Sahara

The Sahel is a region south of the Sahara Desert in Africa where there is very little rainfall. In the 1950s, people moved into this area and began grazing livestock on the scarce plants there. They also burned woodlands to create areas for crops. Years of drought turned the unprotected soil to dust, which blew away on the wind. As a result, the Sahara Desert has expanded 40 kilometers (25 miles) south. In parts of the Sahel, however, replanting is helping to restore the land.

In recent years, the Sahel has suffered terrible droughts, which some experts link to global warming.

WORD BANK
barren producing no life
desertification when grazing animals strip existing plant life, making the land barren
erosion when rock or soil is worn away by the action of the wind, running water, or ice
fertilizer chemical that farmers use to make plants grow better

19

Living World

Plants, animals, and fungi (such as molds) provide people with food, medicines, and materials for clothing and construction. However, by overusing these **resources** from the living world, we threaten Earth's **biodiversity**, meaning its variety of life.

What would YOU do ?

Both people and wildlife need space to thrive. If towns and cities cannot expand, it often causes overcrowding and **pollution**, which affects people's quality of life. However, expanding cities move into wild habitats. Imagine you work for a local government and you need to help developers find space for 1,000 new homes. Where is the best place to build?

Habitats and evolution

A **habitat** is a particular place, such as a woodland or coral reef, that supports certain types of wildlife. Living things are suited to particular conditions in their habitat, such as temperature and kinds of plant life.

Species (specific groups of living things) evolve, or change, in response to changes in their habitat. This process happens gradually, over many generations. However, humans are now bringing rapid change to habitats worldwide. This rapid change makes it difficult for some living things to keep up with the change, putting some species at risk.

Habitat loss

As human **populations** rise, people need more land to grow food, as well as more spaces where they can live and work. Wild grasslands are converted to farmland. Marshes are drained to build new roads, towns, and airports. Mines are opened in remote places such as deserts and Arctic islands. Wild stretches of coast become vacation resorts. As a result, habitats are lost.

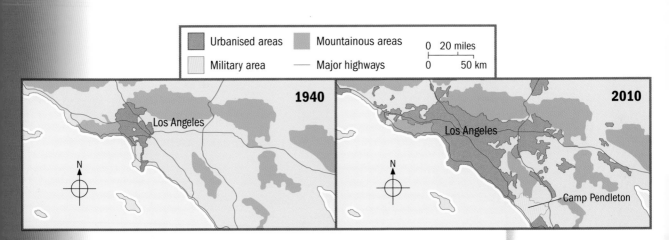

▓ Urbanised areas	▓ Mountainous areas	0 20 miles
░ Military area	— Major highways	0 50 km

1940

Los Angeles

N

2010

Los Angeles

Camp Pendleton

N

These simplified maps show how **urban** (city) areas can expand, particularly along major roads.

Lost prairie

Before the 1800s, the Great Plains of the United States were covered with millions of acres of prairie, meaning flat, largely treeless areas of grassland. These prairies were natural habitats for many species of plants and wildlife, especially prairie birds. However, starting in the mid-1800s, the prairies were plowed up as the U.S. population spread westward in search of areas to settle and grow crops. As a result, much of this wild habitat was lost.

Today, groups like the American Prairie Foundation are working to restore some of these lost habitats. Their work includes reintroducing plants, creating new channels for water, and restocking native fish.
You can read more about their efforts at www.americanprairie.org.

The once-wild grasslands of the U.S. prairies have been plowed up to grow crops.

Clearing forests

Forests cover around 30 percent of Earth's land area. Tropical rain forests have the greatest biodiversity of any habitat, supporting half of all land species.

Local people have lived in the world's forests for thousands of years. Forest resources include timber and wood used for building and fuel, plant and animal foods, rubber, medicines, and **minerals**. Forests are also important to the health of the whole planet because they absorb carbon dioxide and give off oxygen. They form a natural store for carbon, which is released as carbon dioxide when forests are burned—a major cause of **global warming**.

Deforestation

Scientists estimate that 45 percent of the world's rain forests have been cut down since 1850. Forests are logged for their valuable hardwood. Forestland is also cleared to make way for roads, settlements, mines, dams, farms, and cattle ranches. Experts estimate that around 116,000 square kilometers (44,800 square miles) of tropical forest are cut down each year. That is an area the size of 2,400 soccer fields every hour.

Deforestation (the clearing of forestland) is **endangering** thousands of plant and animal species. Current rates of deforestation are not **sustainable**, because there would be little forest left by 2100.

Logging companies say forests are a **renewable** resource, since trees can be replanted. But **environmentalists** say that "old-growth forests" (forests with very old trees), which sustain the most wildlife, take hundreds of years to grow.

About 700,000 square kilometers (270,300 square miles) of the Amazon rain forest were cut down between 1970 and 2008.

Deforestation in Malaysia

Deforestation is happening faster in Malaysia, in Southeast Asia, than in any other rain forest region. About 140,000 hectares (418,500 acres) of Malaysian forests have been cut down each year since 2000. The Malaysian government has come under pressure from environmental groups to stop the logging, which is adding to global warming. Malaysia responds that it needs the money from logging to develop its **industries** and to provide higher standards of living for its people.

Species such as the orangutan are endangered by deforestation in Malaysia.

Why are forests valuable?

People value forests for different reasons:

- To local people, forests have been their families' homes for generations.
- To logging, mining, and other companies, forests are a source of income.
- To governments, forests provide valuable things to **export** (sell to other countries).
- To environmentalists, forests keep the planet healthy.

Which viewpoint is closest to your own?

Fishing

In the 1900s, modern fishing fleets developed technology such as satellites that helped them locate fish. Deep-sea boats called trawlers now sweep their huge nets along the bottom of the sea, capturing 100 tonnes (100 tons) of fish at a time.

For many nations, fishing is a highly profitable industry that supports many people. International fishing fleets travel thousands of miles to reach the best fishing grounds.

Overfishing

Over 90 million tonnes (100 million tons) of fish are caught annually worldwide. These levels are not sustainable. If they continue, the seas will be fished out. Modern fishing methods are so effective that fish such as Atlantic cod and Pacific tuna are now scarce.

The International Council for the Exploration of the Seas reports that around 75 percent of global fish stocks are either fully exploited or overfished. **Overfishing** occurs when so many fish are taken that not enough are left to breed. Since the 1990s, overfishing of small species such as sand eels and anchovies has had an impact on other marine hunters, such as seals and seabirds. In addition, seals, dolphins, and turtles can get trapped in fishing nets and drown.

Fortunately, many nations are now acting to preserve fish stocks by setting limits called quotas on the national fish catch. Nets are also being designed with hatches that allow creatures such as dolphins to escape.

These Pacific tuna are on sale in a Japanese market. Overfishing is making this species scarce.

Dolphins need to surface regularly to breathe. This one has drowned after getting caught in a fishing net.

CASE STUDY

Collapse of the Newfoundland cod industry

Cod were once abundant in the seas around Newfoundland, in Canada. But starting in the 1950s, these waters were heavily fished by factory trawlers from Europe and Asia.

In 1976 Canada banned foreign fishing fleets, but continued to harvest 250,000 tonnes (275,500 tons) of cod a year itself. Experts warned of the danger of overfishing, but were ignored. In 1992 Newfoundland cod stocks crashed. The industry closed, causing the loss of 40,000 jobs. Despite the fishing ban, cod have not recovered in the area.

Biodiversity

Earth has great biodiversity. About 1.75 million species of plants and animals have been identified so far. Unfortunately, scientists estimate that about 50 species become extinct (die out) a day. That is two every hour.

Hunting and the pet trade

Habitat loss is a major cause of species dying out. Hunting is another factor. In **developing countries** in Africa, wild animals are sometimes killed for meat. They are also targeted for their hides, fur, tusks, and other body parts, which are traded internationally.

Some species are captured for sale as pets. The trade in live animals has boomed since the 1990s because of the Internet, which makes it easier for collectors to locate animals for sale. Many creatures die during transportation, or soon after they are sold because their owners do not provide the right conditions.

Protecting rare species

Most countries now have laws to protect endangered wildlife. More than 150 countries have signed an agreement called the Convention on International Trade in Endangered Species, which bans trade in threatened wildlife. But rare animals fetch high prices on the illegal market, and some people are still prepared to risk heavy fines to catch and sell them.

This warehouse in Honduras is full of crocodile skins ready for export. The skins will be made into expensive items such as purses, belts, and shoes.

European wildlife trade

The European Union (EU) **imports** (buys from other countries) more wildlife products than any other place in the world. The legal wildlife trade is a multibillion-dollar industry, and the illegal trade is growing rapidly. In 2003 to 2004, EU customs officers seized 7,000 illegal shipments, including tropical hardwoods, crocodile skins, snakeskins, and live lizards and snakes.

Every year, customs officers seize smuggled wildlife and animal products worth millions of dollars.

Population and Resources

Today, rich and poor nations consume very unequal shares of Earth's **resources**. In wealthy countries, we use enormous amounts of resources, while in places like Africa, people get by with very little. According to the United Nations **Population** Fund, the wealthiest countries of the world make up just 20 percent of the world's total population, but they consume 86 percent of Earth's resources.

Wasteful world

In **developed countries** such as the United States, we enjoy a comfortable lifestyle. Our homes are full of machines and gadgets such as refrigerators, televisions, and laptops. All this technology is made available by **fossil fuels** and other resources. We also end up throwing away a lot of what we buy quite quickly, including huge amounts of packaging. This way of life helps to drive the economy. However, it also involves a lot of waste.

In the world's richest nations, we spend money on a huge range of products.

Developing world

In the last 20 years or so, **developing countries** such as China and India have quickly started to develop **industries**. As more nations go in this direction, more resources and energy are used, increasing the world's **ecological footprint**.

"The world contains enough resources for everyone's need, but not for everyone's greed"
Indian leader, Mahatma Gandhi

People in developing countries look to the lifestyle of the West, and so they want cars, computers, and all the other things that make life comfortable — and who can blame them? However, the rising use of energy and resources in India, China, and other developing countries is adding to problems such as air **pollution** and **climate change**.

High-tech industries such as car manufacturing are now thriving in developing nations such as India.

CASE STUDY

Lithium mining in Bolivia

Poor countries have the right to profit from their own resources. However, if **multinational** companies fund the development of operations such as mining, they often take most of the profit.

For example, huge, untapped reserves of a metal called lithium have been located in Bolivia, in South America. Lithium is used in new fuel-efficient vehicle batteries. Multinational corporations are trying to take control of mining operations in Bolivia, to gain a valuable raw material at a low price. It is unlikely that Bolivia will be able to use its own **mineral** wealth to escape from poverty.

Rising populations

The world's population is currently rising by some 75 million people each year. Most of this expansion is taking place in developing countries, where there are fewer resources and often less land that is good for growing crops. This places a great strain on the environment. It also causes widespread hardship. Over a billion people—nearly one-sixth of the world's population—struggle to live on less than a dollar a day.

Seeking better opportunities and jobs, many people in developing countries move to cities. However, when large numbers of people move into a city from the country, it can challenge a city's ability to provide services such as waste disposal. Many people also end up homeless.

Food and hunger

Experts say the world's farmers are able to grow enough food to feed everyone. But at the moment, this is not happening. The richest 30 percent of the world's population consumes 60 percent of the world's food. Meanwhile, 935 million people, most living in the world's poorest countries, do not get enough to eat.

"The right to food is fundamental to human existence."
United Nations Food and Agriculture Organization

In developing countries such as Kenya, many people in cities end up living on the street or in makeshift slums called shantytowns.

In the United States, roughly half of the population is overweight, while just 4 percent is malnourished.

Wasting food

In developed countries, many people buy more food than they need and end up throwing it away. In the United States, one quarter of all food is wasted.

Western diets involve a lot of meat. But raising livestock such as beef cattle uses far more resources, such as land, water, and nutrients, than is needed to grow crops. Scientists have calculated that the land needed to raise the cattle to feed 5 people could feed 150 people if a crop such as maize were planted instead.

CASE STUDY

Hamburgers or rain forests?

Hamburgers are a popular fast food in the West. Over 20 ingredients, such as beef, wheat, lettuce, tomatoes, onions, and mayonnaise, go into, or are served with, every hamburger. Some of these products are bought from developing countries. In the United States, a lot of the beef used in hamburgers comes from cattle raised on ranches in Brazil, in South America. Tropical rain forests are cut down to clear land for cattle ranching to raise this meat.

The global economy

Today, the world's nations are closely linked through trade. A high percentage of the goods in our stores come from fast-developing nations such as India and China. However, transporting goods across the world by airplane, ship, and truck uses huge amounts of energy and is a major cause of air pollution, since fossil fuels are burned as fuel.

When multinational companies set the prices, local growers earn very little.

Imports and exports

Much of the food we buy in supermarkets also comes from developing countries in regions such as Africa. The governments of food-producing nations need the income from **exporting** these so-called "cash crops" to pay for **imports** such as machinery.

However, the trade is usually controlled by large multinational companies, which give farmers a low price for their produce. In addition, the multinational companies often get to use the best land for themselves, leaving poor farmers with semi-**barren** land to raise crops to feed their families.

Flying fruits and vegetables all the way from the tropics gives Western shoppers a wide choice, but it is a huge waste of fuel.

Fair trade

The fair trade movement is helping to give farmers in developing countries a better deal. As part of this movement, developed countries establish trading partnerships with developing countries. The goal is to achieve fair prices and good working conditions for farmers in poorer parts of the world. For their part, growers must produce high-quality produce without damaging the environment.

Fair trade covers a wide range of goods, including bananas, coffee, tea, cocoa, and sugar cane. Fair trade products are usually a little more expensive, but the extra money is passed on to farmers in developing countries. You can look for the fair trade sticker on items you buy in the supermarket.

Find out more

The next time you visit the supermarket, examine labels on produce to find out the country of origin. Use a map to work out roughly how far the goods have traveled. Which product has the most "food miles" (the distance traveled to get to you, the consumer)? Look for fair trade labels on products, too.

CASE STUDY

Two-way traffic

Scientists studying the movement of imports and exports have discovered that international trade quite often involves a pointless, two-way traffic of almost identical goods. For example, in 2006 the United Kingdom exported 21 tonnes (23 tons) of bottled mineral water to Australia and imported 20 tonnes (22 tons) of Australian mineral water. What a waste!

Sustainable Living

Sustainability is a challenge the world must address. By 2050 the world **population** will have grown by another two to three billion people. Earth can provide the **resources** to support this number of people only if we change our habits. Simply carrying on with our wasteful Western lifestyle will cause lasting damage to the planet and lead to severe shortages of food, water, timber, fuel, and other essential resources.

Many people are now aware of the need to live more sustainably, and to make sure there are enough resources for all. But how exactly can it be done?

Earth summits

In 1992 the world's nations met at the Earth Summit in Rio de Janeiro, Brazil, to discuss these issues. Wealthy and poor nations agreed on a strategy for **sustainable development**. This breakthrough included a **Climate Change** Convention to tackle **global warming**, as well as a **Biodiversity** Convention to preserve the natural world.

The Japanese Prime Minister gives a speech at the Millennium Development Goals Summit in 2010.

In 2000 sustainability was a key issue at the United Nations Millennium Summit. At this meeting, 192 world leaders signed the Millennium Declaration, pledging to maintain biodiversity, improve education and health in **developing countries**, and halve the number of people living in poverty by 2015.

The way forward

Since then, national and local governments worldwide have introduced measures to cut waste and **pollution**. For example, cities have introduced new, low-pollution modes of public transportation. They offer companies that introduce **sustainable** working methods benefits such as tax breaks.

We cannot leave it all to governments, however. It is up to each and every one of us to live less wastefully and reduce our own, personal **ecological footprint**.

Bike-rental projects, such as this one in Taipei, Taiwan, are encouraging people to use bycicles, rather than cars or buses, for short journeys around cities.

What would YOU do ?

Governments pass laws aimed at encouraging us to live more sustainably. However, such moves can be unpopular. Imagine you are a government official with the task of reducing air pollution caused by cars. One way to do this is to raise taxes on fuel. If gasoline is more expensive, people will probably use cars less, which will cut air pollution. The money raised could be used to improve public transportation. However, the tax will be unpopular with voters, and maybe with businesses, too. It could even cost you the next election. What would you do?

Find out more

The United Nations Environment Program recommends that 10 percent of each country's land should be set aside and protected from development. Countries such as Austria, Ecuador, and the Netherlands exceed the target, while Russia and Egypt fall short. Find out how your country measures up by logging onto http://mdgs.un.org/unsd/mdg/Data.aspx.

Conservation

Conservation is action taken to protect the natural world and wildlife. It safeguards key resources such as forests and biodiversity. Conservationists say the best way to protect wildlife is to protect whole **habitats** by establishing wildlife reserves and national parks. For example, in 1872 the U.S. government set up the world's first national park in Yellowstone, Wyoming. Since then, nations around the world have followed suit. There are now over 110,000 protected areas worldwide, covering 12 percent of Earth's land area.

Sustainable parks

Some reserves are vast, remote wilderness areas. Whether large or small, reserves need to be managed carefully to conserve resources and avoid harm to nature. Mining and development are kept to a minimum or outlawed altogether.

Some parks receive large numbers of visitors, which can bring problems such as overcrowding, litter, and path **erosion**. The authorities must find ways to manage these pressures (see box at right).

The Northeast Greenland National Park, in Greenland, is the world's largest reserve, covering 972,000 square kilometers (375,300 square miles).

A park ranger describes the biodiversity of Saguaro National Park in Arizona. Providing information about nature is a key function of parks and reserves.

Sustainable forestry

The world's forests are a crucial resource, important not only to the nations concerned but also to the health of the whole planet. Forests can be managed sustainably by selecting only certain trees for cutting, and by planting saplings to replace trees that are cut down. Forests can also be managed sustainably by harvesting products such as rubber and Brazil nuts without cutting down trees.

CASE STUDY

Park management in Yosemite National Park

Yosemite National Park, located in California, is one of the most popular national parks in the United States. It is known for its beautiful cliffs, waterfalls, and Giant Sequoia trees.

Services for tourists such as campsites, restaurants, and bus services are all located together in a relatively small area. This leaves almost 95 percent of the park as open wilderness, where hundreds of **species** of plants and animals are able to thrive. This also reduces the spread of negative impacts of tourism, such as litter and traffic congestion. Find out more about Yosemite at http://www.yosemite.national-park.com.

Preserving environmental resources

Soil and water are key environmental resources. However, as we have seen, modern farming practices are overstraining and damaging these resources.

Sustainable farming allows farmers to harvest crops while maintaining the health of the soil, water, and environment. **Organic** farming is a method of farming that does not use chemicals. Organic farmers use natural **fertilizers** such as manure to nourish crops. Pests such as aphids may be controlled through natural predators such as ladybugs. The practice of crop rotation (growing different crops each year) helps to keep the soil healthy.

Planting deep-rooted crops and hedges can help to restore land that is suffering from **desertification** or erosion. Steep hillsides can be terraced (cut into steps) to retain both soil and water.

Water conservation

Over-**extraction** of water is threatening farming in many regions, from Africa to Australia. In the next few decades, climate change is likely to make these problems worse. Farmers can conserve water by using efficient **irrigation** techniques rather than wasteful sprinkler systems. A technique called desalination can be used to convert seawater to freshwater. However, desalination is expensive, and only wealthy nations can afford it. It is far cheaper to conserve existing supplies—for example, by fixing leaks.

The practice of "intercropping" (growing several crops in one field) helps to restore nutrients in the soil.

Make a problem-solving model

A diagram called a problem-solving model can help you organize your research about complex issues such as good farming practices. The key question goes in the problem box. The boxes below set out possible solutions and their consequences. Use the example shown here to summarize your research. Now make a similar model about water conservation.

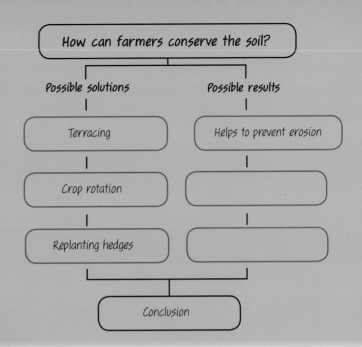

How can farmers conserve the soil?

Possible solutions | Possible results

Terracing → Helps to prevent erosion

Crop rotation

Replanting hedges

Conclusion

Water conservation in Israel

Israel is a dry country where technology is helping farmers to conserve water. In a technique called drip irrigation, a network of pipes delivers moisture directly to crop roots.

Sometimes too much irrigation causes a build-up of natural salts in the soil. This problem, called salinization, can also be a problem in dry countries. Farmers are overcoming this by developing salt-resistant varieties of grapes and tomatoes. They are also avoiding crops, such as rice, that require a lot of water.

This drip irrigation system is being used to water young plants.

Sustainable solutions

Sustainability is a huge challenge that must be faced, not only by scientists, politicians, and businesses, but also by ordinary people. We all need to make changes in our lives to sustain Earth's resources and make sure everyone gets a fair share of them, both now and in the future.

Saving energy and water at home

The energy we use at home is mostly created by using harmful **fossil fuels**. But we do not need to use as much energy. There are literally hundreds of ways to conserve energy. The simplest is to switch off lights and machines when you are not using them. Taking a shower instead of a bath reduces the energy used to heat water and also conserves water, as does only running dishwashers and washing machines when they are full.

Reducing pollution

Burning fossil fuels causes harmful air pollution. The simplest way for most of us to reduce pollution is to use cars less and public transportation more. Buying local produce from stores and markets helps to reduce pollution from the "air miles" created by having these goods transported. It also saves energy. Look for organic foods or, better still, grow your own!

Recycling materials such as glass saves energy and natural resources.

Tackling waste

Following the "three Rs" of waste disposal— reduce, reuse, and recycle—cuts pollution and energy use. Do not buy goods with too much packaging. Reuse plastic bags and containers. If you have a compost facility nearby, recycle food scraps there. Recycling bottles, cans, paper, cardboard, and plastic conserves natural resources such as **minerals**, metals, oil, and timber. Simple measures like these can really help to sustain the resources on which we all depend.

What would YOU do?

Find out more about the United Nations' Millennium Development Goals by visiting www.undp.org/mdg/basics.shtml. Eight main goals for living more sustainably are listed (see page 43). What would your top three priorities be, and why?

CASE STUDY

Sustainable cities

Over half the world's population now lives in **urban** areas. By 2050 it is likely to be two-thirds of the population. Rapidly growing cities draw heavily on local resources such as timber, food, and water. They also suffer from pollution.

Many cities worldwide are now putting in place sustainable solutions that clean up the environment and improve living conditions. For example, many local governments are investing in non-polluting transportation. Land that has been built on before is also being reused for development instead of green spaces. And guidelines and tax breaks are making it easier for people to make their homes energy-efficient.

Solar panels on the roof of an apartment block in Paris, France, provide energy for the people who live there.

41

Facts and Figures

Ecological footprints

This table shows the top 10 nations with the highest **ecological footprint** per person (measured as the amount of land needed to provide **resources** for one person).

Ranking	Country	Hectares (acres) needed to provide resources per person
1.	United Arab Emirates	15.99 (39.51)
2.	United States	12.22 (30.20)
3.	Kuwait	10.31 (25.48)
4.	Denmark	9.88 (24.41)
5.	New Zealand	9.54 (23.57)
6.	Ireland	9.43 (23.30)
7.	Australia	8.49 (20.98)
8.	Finland	8.45 (20.88)
9.	Canada	7.66 (18.93)
10.	Sweden	7.53 (18.61)

Source: www.nationmaster.com/graph/env_eco_foo-environment-ecological-footprint

Fishing

The top five countries with the largest fish catch.

Ranking	Country	Size of catch in tonnes (tons)
1.	China	10,433,170 (11,500,600)
2.	Peru	7,490,730 (8,257,120)
3.	Chile	4,433,240 (4,886,810)
4.	Japan	3,593,660 (3,961,330)
5.	Russia	3,145,380 (3,467,190)

Source: www.nationmaster.com/graph/env_mar_fis_cat-environment-marine-fish-catch

Developed land

The top five countries with the greatest percentage of developed land.

Ranking	Country	Percentage of total land area that is developed
1.	Belgium	43.93
2.	Netherlands	43.79
3.	Denmark	39.45
4.	Germany	32.84
5.	United Kingdom	32.05

Source: www.nationmaster.com/graph/env_non_wil-environment-non-wildness

Wilderness

The top five countries with the greatest percentage of wilderness.

Ranking	Country	Percentage of wilderness
1.	Libya	89.90
2.	Canada	81.87
3.	Algeria	80.82
4.	Iceland	80.08
5.	Mauritania	79.46

Source: www.nationmaster.com/graph/env_wil-environment-wildness

United Nations Millennium Development Goals

1. Eradicate [end] extreme poverty and hunger. Halve the proportion of people living on less than $1 a day, and halve the proportion of people who suffer from hunger by 2015.

2. Achieve universal primary education.

3. Promote gender equality and empower women.

4. Reduce Child Mortality Rate [the number of children who die].

5. Improve maternal health [the health of pregnant women].

6. Combat HIV/AIDS, malaria, and other diseases.

7. Ensure environmental sustainability, reduce biodiversity loss.

8. Develop a global partnership for development.

Source: www.undp.org/mdg/basics.shtml

Glossary

aquifer layer of rock or earth underground that holds water

atmosphere envelope of gases that surrounds Earth

barren producing little to no plant life

biodiversity variety of life in a particular habitat

climate change change in the regular weather patterns of a region

conservation work done to protect the natural world

deforestation when forestland is cleared of trees

desertification when grazing animals strip existing plant life, making the land barren

developed country wealthy country where people have a high standard of living

developing country country where people do not have a high standard of living

drought severe and long-lasting lack of water in a region

ecological footprint measure of human demands on Earth's resources. This term is sometimes also called a "global footprint."

endanger put at risk of extinction (dying out)

environmentalist person who works to help the environment

erosion when rock or soil is worn away by the action of wind, running water, or ice

export sell and transport something to another country

extract remove from the earth

fertilizer chemical that farmers use to make plants grow better

flow resource natural force that derives energy from movement, such as winds, tides, and rivers

fossil fuel fuel, such as coal, oil, and natural gas, that is made of fossilized plants or animals that lived millions of years ago

global warming rising temperatures worldwide, caused by an increase of gases in the atmosphere that trap the Sun's heat

greenhouse effect warming effect caused by certain gases in the air, which prevent some of the Sun's heat from escaping into space

habitat particular place that sustains certain types of wildlife

import buy in goods from another country

industry type of work that creates something to be sold, often through the use of factories and power plants

irrigation method of controlling the flow of water through channels and other devices

mineral hard, naturally occurring substance. Minerals help provide everything from cement to gold.

multinational operating in several countries

nonrenewable describes resources, such as coal or oil, that will get used up

organic method of farming that does not use chemicals

overfishing when so many fish are taken that not enough are left to breed

pollution when the natural world is harmed by waste or by any substance that does not belong there

population number of people in an area

renewable describes a resource that will not get used up

resource something that is useful or valuable

species specific group of living things

sustainability using Earth's resources in a planned and careful way

sustainable when resources are managed so that they will not run out in the future, causing little damage to the environment

sustainable development managing economic growth and the way we live, without destroying resources that will be needed for the future

tailings waste rock left over from mining

toxic poisonous

urban relating to the city

Find Out More

Books

Belmont, Helen. *Planning for a Sustainable Future (Geography Skills)*. Mankato, Minn.: Smart Apple Media, 2008.

Calhoun, Yael, ed. *Conservation (Environmental Issues)*. Philadelphia: Chelsea House, 2005.

Gorman, Jacqueline Laks. *Fossil Fuels (What If We Do Nothing?)*. Pleasantville, N.Y.: Gareth Stevens, 2009.

Green, Jen. *Reducing Air Pollution (Improving Our Environment)*. Milwaukee: Gareth Stevens, 2005.

Green, Jen. *Saving Water (Improving Our Environment)*. Milwaukee: Gareth Stevens, 2005.

Jakab, Cheryl. *Sustainable Cities (Global Issues)*. Mankato, Minn.: Smart Apple Media, 2010.

Rooney, Anne. *Sustainable Water Resources (How Can We Save Our World?)*. Mankato, Minn.: Arcturus, 2010.

Senker, Cath. *Sustainable Transportation (How Can We Save Our World?)*. Mankato, Minn.: Arcturus, 2010.

Simon, Seymour. *Global Warming*. New York: Harper Collins, 2010.

Solway, Andrew. *Environmental Technology (New Technology)*. Mankato, Minn.: Smart Apple Media, 2009.

Spilsbury, Richard. *The Great Outdoors: Saving Habitats (You Can Save the Planet)*. Chicago: Heinemann Library, 2005.

Websites

www.footprintnetwork.org/en/index.php/GFN/page/earth_overshoot_day/
Learn more about ecological footprints at this Global Footprint Network website.

http://ase.org/programs/green-schools-program
Learn how the Alliance to Save Energy is trying to make schools more environmentally friendly with its "Green Schools" program.

www.epa.gov/kids/air.htm
This website of the U.S. Environmental Protection Agency provides facts about air pollution, including links that discuss climate change.

www.eere.energy.gov/kids/
This website, created by the U.S. Department of Energy Efficiency and Renewable Energy, offers games, tips, and facts to help young people save energy.

www.unfpa.org/public/
Learn more about what the United Nations Population Fund is doing to help improve the lives of people around the world.

www.wateraidamerica.org
Learn more about ways people are trying to get freshwater to all parts of the world at this Water Aid website.

www.nps.gov/index.htm
Learn more about nature reserves at the U.S. National Park Service website.

www.greenpeace.org/usa/
Learn more about what the environmental group Greenpeace is doing to protect the environment.

www.foe.org
Learn more about how the environmental group Friends of the Earth is trying to save the environment.

www.worldwildlife.org /home-full.html
Learn more about the efforts of the World Wide Fund (WWF).

Index